Small Comforts

Mareska Chettiar

BookLeaf Publishing

Presentation by *BookLeaf Publishing*

Web: www.bookleafpub.com

E-mail: info@bookleafpub.com

ISBN: 9789357697576

First edition 2023

To Thatha. Thank you for always believing in me.

PREFACE

It's a beautiful time
When someone walks into your life
And suddenly everything has color again.

New Soil

In moments like these, I turn to my paper.
How else could I describe this void,
If not through poetry?

How else can I describe the moment I am uprooted,
Stolen, pushed, forced,
Into new soil, wall away from familiarity
Well away from warmth?

How else can I describe being a stranger—
With no place of belonging, and no home?

In new soil I am abandoned.
In new soil I am cold.

And yet the world remains relentless,
Forcing me along a path.
Through the hurdles,
Through the soil that chips at my resilience.

I knew the warmth would never hurt me,
I would dwell in the memories and comforting familiarity,
In the knowledge that I would be protected.

But I awake in chipping soil,
Drowning in a warmth long gone.

I should accept my reality.
I should accept where I stand.
And adapt to the soil I stand on.

And soon, I will question which soil was
chipping,
For in new soil I am familiar,
In new soil I am kept.

The Passing of a Moment

A light breeze blows.
Calm. Patient.
It brings joy and warmth.
Summer is a fleeting feeling.

To Someone I've Never Seen

My heart sings a lonely song,
But you somehow keep along
Ahead of me, easily
While I struggle to keep up pace
But alas, I'm quite based.

Why don't you get out of my head?
Leave me some peace in your stead?
My love is so scared
Of being open and bared
Yet you seem so unaware.

Though how much I miss you
I wouldn't dare say I'd kiss you
Those nights we spent were all a lie,
When you left me alone, to die.

In the dark, buried deep inside,
I said goodbye
And didn't cry.

Fine Lines

Some things make me laugh,
So much that my stomach hurts,
Inside a dead silent library.
Some make me cry,
Alone and desperate,
Inside a dead silent library.
Some things grip my neck and don't let go,
So much that breathing hurts,
Inside a dead silent library.
Some things make me pause in contemplation,
Or wallow in desecration,
Inside a dead silent library.
And some fill me with this giddy feeling,
Like love but not quite that deep,
More like a longing for something intoxicating
Impossible outside finely printed lines
Inside a dead silent library.

I'm (Not) an Academic Weapon. And it Hurts.

Why do my failures weigh on me so?
The unrequited love that wraps around my hear
Like a leeching thorny vines
On a century-old tree.
The academics overwhelm me,
Drowning me in a sea of things left undone,
As I struggle to satisfy expectations.
Why must life make me suffer so?
Why must I live in a time
Where individuality shrinks,
And your worth is solely based on memory tests and attention spans?
How can I survive?
How can my heart survive?
True comfort is scarce,
Just like true fidelity,
Lives are discarded, discredited and denied
Prayers remain a whisper unanswered
And I wait, crying,
And I wait, standing,
And I wait for a life not possible in my time,
And I stand.

Long Nights

I hear the hum of machinery,
The soft noise I don't notice
When the world is up and running.

I see the shadows move across my wall,
With a mystery that I examine not,
When I stay occupied with work unending.

I feel the droop of my eyes,
A slight burn that I ignore,
When people do the tasks still pending.

I hear my heart thud in my ears,
A familiar but overlooked melody,
When I lie with the world, waiting.

I feel the weight of the blanket,
Warm but convenient,
When I hide, unstressing.

I think about these little feelings,
Unimportant things that make life serene,
When I await slumber at night, relaxing.

I Have This Big Bucket of Love in Me and Sometimes it Overflows

Sometimes you just need some love,
Because there hasn't been a problem
That love couldn't solve.
When uncertainty weighs on you,
You fall back on that feeling
And it stands like a steady trunk—
Silent, unmoving, patient,
For you, who it praises like a diety.

That love is precious, transcending
Space and time and complications,
Returning to simplicity
When you need it the most.
Love is irrational,
And love is strong.
And more of it, sometimes,
Is all that is needed.

An Ancestry of Womanhood

I am my mother.
And I am my mother's mother.
And all the mothers before that.

They all trickle down into me,
Little bits and pieces and memories,
That make me the woman I am today.

I am the fruit of unimaginable suffering and
pain,
But receive love like no other,
As if I were a testament to their strength.

I am my mother's daughter,
And my grandmother's legacy.
I remember their strife.

I remember their pain,
Their tears and blood,
Their forced smiles and gestures.

I remember.
I acknowledge the atrocities
The unforgivable crimes against them.

They lived, and they loved.
They made me unshakeable like them.
And I will not forget.

A Small Glow I Noticed That Never Fades

A person's worth shines,
A bright glow I cannot ignore,
And I look upon them
With tenderness and love,
And treat them
With nothing but kindness.
They may be lost,
They may be struggling,
But their worth remains constant
An unshakeable glow,
That they themselves cannot perceive.
And so I stay,
Reminding them of that brightness.
It might not be my job,
But these tiny glows are too precious
To be ignored and forgotten,
Especially by their people.

A Realization that I Don't Know What to Make Of

It leaves slowly,
Ebbing away almost unnoticed.
And one day,
You suddenly realize it's gone,
And wonder what happened to it.
While you sort out the complexities,
You find there wasn't a single instance,
No, not just one—
But a thousand, maybe more
Over months, maybe decades
That slowly chipped at it.
And you shrug,
Realizing you're above worrying.
Of course, you care,
Of course, you love.
You will cry at their funeral,
Say your condolences,
And take your place.
You will realize that love still exists,
In all its complexity,
But the respect has long since left.
And once again, you will shrug,
Accept the pain and void,
And reiterate the cycle of growth.
Because you're grown up now.

A Stooge

I used to watch the leaves blow,
And watch the rain trail down my window.
It was calm. Peaceful.
There was nothing more to nature
Than nature itself,
And I relished in that comfort
Knowing it would not hurt me.
And then people came along.
With their problems and complexities,
Desires and greed.
I stayed constant,
And catered to them with kindness,
But they pointed out all the flaws in me,
All that they did not think fit in
With their social construct.
And so I was ostracized,
When all I did was show kindness,
And I was shunned,
When I said nothing.
Yet I remained constant,
Keeping faith,
Because there must be more to being human.

Sometimes It's Me Against the World

If I took a small venture
Into the very depths of my mind,
I would find wonderful things.
Happy memories long forgotten,
Smells and tastes and feelings,
Hugs and laughter and love,
Sweet, wholesome memories.
I would also find pain,
Loss and grief and discomfort,
Lessons and mistakes and regret,
Tearful, shameful memories.
And if I continued to venture,
I would look into my very core,
My heart, my mind and soul,
To see what makes me whole.
And again, past everything,
The love and grief and pain,
I would find something wonderful—
Myself.

The Fight Passes

My heart sinks.
Screams are still ringing in my ear.
Tears streak down my face,
And I do nothing to stop them.
Hiding tears is shameful,
More than crying itself.
I will not allow myself to be weak.
But my heart is screaming.

I Hope You Have A Good Life

The years have passed and we've grown older
But I really still can't get over
Those four words that define us.
You should be honored!
Time hasn't withered my curiosity
Nor that memory so fragile
And you continue to stroll in and out of my life
Leaving me broken, frustrated and belied.
Why do we keep encountering each other?
Why can't the universe just end my suffering
And let you out of my sight?
Why must I be tormented so?
The fun is lost, as is the fascination
All that is left are thoughts unsaid
With no consolation.
I want to communicate, I really do,
But I deserve better, so my words I chew.
Why don't the feelings go away?
This isn't fair, or okay.
You seem different, a little conflicted
But I don't miss the way our eyes meet,
The way they did all those years ago,
When the time was right,
And we had room to grow
Before those words—four.

I Think I Fell In Love

They say beauty lies in the eyes of the beholder
But what happens when those eyes
Transcend beauty itself?
The cosmos couldn't compete with the depth,
Nor could the Bid Bang with the colors.
If God exists, let me ask them
How could you expect me to worship you,
When religions could fall behind those solemn orbs?
When grand civilizations could rise and surge
Under those ghastly, perfect chasms?
Alas, I cannot look into them.
Not because they are too intimidating—
But because they were too soft,
Kind and ancient,
Something I must treasure.
But you get lost in treasure, lost in greed.
And if I looked in, I would never look away.
Into those trapping, lovely, lovely sweet mysteries.
They say eyes are the windows to the soul
But what might happen
If the eyes were souls themselves?

This Was a Breakdown, If You Couldn't Tell

The words spill out uncontrollably,
And my palm bleeds as my fingers bite into it
Ever so painfully.
What is happening to me?
On the outside I live a normal life,
Yet the nights I spend crying myself to sleep
Say otherwise.
And the years pass and I wither on the inside,
Keeping all the feelings locked away,
The tears, frustration and anger,
No one can see it!
I'm an absolute embarrassment,
And everyone knows.
My energy and social life are gone,
I'm now but a shell of what I used to be—
Happy, content and carefree.
But I don't know what those words mean
anymore.
My goals lay abandoned,
Just like the people I love,
I while away my time
In a world that doesn't seem like mine
Running, screaming, crying away my
responsibilities

Because I'm not who I used to be.
And maybe I'm cowardly, weak and undisciplined,
And maybe I'm living life
As half of what it's meant to be,
But that's okay!
Because we all die anyway.

Beauty

You look in the mirror and see someone.
Surprise is etched on their face,
Like they couldn't believe they looked at all.
That surprise turns into curiosity,
And it was like they were seeing
Something foreign—strange.

They continued looking,
Even touched the mirror in wonder,
Thinking about how long it had been
Since they last it.

Because it was glowing.
Dancing, even.

And suddenly, the person beamed,
A breathtaking smile appeared
And they seemed to have remembered
Something forgotten in adversity.

They seemed to have remembered
That behind all the pressures,
The hate, the sabotage—
That there exists something
Untouchable.
Terrifying.
And divine.

Sometimes I Feel the Cracks

I always wondered why
I wasn't able to move on.
Was it because I felt too deeply?
Was it because every time I fell in love
I gave them a piece of my soul?

How is it that every time I hear that song,
Or see that phrase,
Or that book they liked—
That missing piece starts to ache,
Reminding me of what I've lost.

But I stay aching, reminiscing,
Because with the pain comes memory,
And even though it makes my eyes water—
And wish the missing piece would come back,
I knew I wouldn't take it back, even if I could.

Who Is She?

This is the story
Of a little loud girl
Who had everything she wanted.

She had a loving family,
An irresistible personality,
And an honest view of the world.

Her childhood was filled with joy and memories,
And she never knew grief or loneliness.

But today, that loud little girl hides.
She's reserved now,
A little shy.

People call her graceful and intelligent,
And she accepts compliments with hesitance.
She doesn't show her genuine smile anymore,
And her honest views are tainted with distrust.

She's known grief. She's known pain.
She's known the darkest depths of loss.
She cries herself to sleep sometimes,
And suffers through the expanse of her feelings.
She's convinced the little loud girl died.

So she doesn't try anymore,
And just smiles.